Oops, I Spilled the Coffee Again!

Oops, I Spilled the Coffee Again!

by Sharon Buck White

CHRISTOS PRESS

Dayton, Washington

Scripture Quotations are taken from the New International Version

Personality Plus by Florence Littauer, referred to in the preface, is published by Fleming H. Revell Company, Old Tappan, New Jersey, copyright 1983.

ISBN 0-945265-00-X

Library of Congress Catalog Card Number 88-70111

Cover and illustrations by Alan White

This book is dedicated to my sister Charm.

Table of Contents

Foreward

Here is a book that won't allow you to put it down, no matter how busy, tired, or uninspired you feel! It takes you places just like where you are right now, and brings you out, sharing the wonderful Father-love of God as he sees every situation we encounter.

Sharon White, daughter of Pastor Roland Buck, (*Angels on Assignment*) has written a book which delves into that hidden part of us which makes us feel like we're a failure, only to discover that God and his loving hand overcome all!

How he takes what we feel are faults and failures and turns them into plus situations will cause you to rise up from any poignant, painful, pungent, intense, piercing predicament or plight and feel the arms of God envelop you.

As a mother forgives her children, and hugs them as she holds them in her arms, Sharon White has done a remarkable job of showing us that particular nature of God.

Whether you are a baby Christian, or a mature one, you will find yourself somewhere in this book.

Charles and Frances Hunter

Preface

I was burned out from trying to measure up to expectations from people who were not like me. I had always accepted myself as being OK, but all of a sudden it seemed I was not OK.

I had been asked to speak for a Women Aglow group in Coeur d'Alene, Idaho, and decided to take an extra day to visit my sister Charm. She lives in Pullman, about two hours from Coeur d'Alene. I arrived at her house tired, joyless, and discouraged. Charm took one look at me and said, "You have to read this book I have. It will help you, Sharon!"

The last thing I wanted to do in this state of mind was read someone else's *great book*, but Charm made me promise. I sighed deeply. I had one day before my speaking engagement, which I felt would be just as dry as I was. I filled the big, old-fashioned tub (it even had legs) to the brim so I could soak while reading.

In just a few pages I started experiencing God's blessings. Suddenly I felt so blessed I leaped out of the bathtub and started walking and reading and praising the Lord. What book was it, you ask? Well, I'm not in the habit of advertising someone else's book before the reader even has a chance to read my first chapter, but the book was *Personality Plus* by Florence Littauer.

Her book reminded me of things I already knew—that God made me the way I am, and it's OK to laugh, to be forgetful, to be friendly, dramatic or silly. It's OK to spill a cup of coffee.

The next day at the Women Aglow meeting, over one hundred ladies experienced a revived, revitalized joyful speaker. The response was tremendous, and I went home and began this little book.

In this book you'll find two portraits. The first is of one of God's kids, who with childlike faith lives life with a flair—that's me! The second portrait is of my Heavenly Father who has picked me up, bandaged my hurt spots, encouraged, loved, and made up the difference in every situation to make my portrait complete.

My husband Alan is a portrait artist, and also a cartoonist. He did all the artwork in this book. But in creating portraits or depicting ideas, many times he has to erase and start over. Yet on the finished artwork, you only see the beauty and perfection.

I hope you will receive a refreshing spirit in your life as you read this little book of joy and hope in Father God who makes the difference.

Acknowledgments

Special thanks to Pat and Ross Casey, who allowed me to invade their home and use their word processor to complete this book, and to Ross again for helping put the pages together. Also thanks to Bob and Sharon Lewandowski, who taught me how to use a word processor and walked through the first draft of this book with me. Thanks to all my encouragers who laughed and cried in all the right places in this book: Marilyn Tucker, Sue Carpenter, Amy Gerla, my mother Charm Buck, my sister Marilyn Fuller, Karen Thorngren, and Dawn Johnson. You blessed me!

Coffee Break

God looked down from his Heaven upon the affairs of mankind, and sighed. Signaling a passing band of angels, he said, "Get a big cleaning cloth and some mops. There's another mess down there to clean up. There's a whole group of people who have spilled their coffee. Follow the trail of coffee stains across the Universe, and wipe them up as you go. Wait! Sharon is in the middle of that group. You'd better grab an extra large mop!"

Then God smiled and said, "I'm the one who designed every one of those spillers. I put my 'treasure in earthern vessels,' and I love every one of those clay pots, especially the ones who are broken and cracked."

Oops, I Spilled the Coffee Again!

I for one am certainly glad God recognizes who we are! The story of my life is that I'm a spiller. I'll confess. I spill milk, Coke, punch, anything that's liquid. But most of all, I spill coffee. It's probably because I walk around with a cup of coffee in my hand talking to people. I leave little coffee trails on floors, and its mark on people. I carry this treasure around, tripping and spilling—imperfect, but with his joy, my strength. This little earthen vessel tries to help God out or runs ahead of him with the cup of her life; ahead of the coffee maker, but still forgiven.

Why not pour yourself a cup of coffee or a tall icy glass of your favorite beverage. Get a plate of your favorite cookies (mine are chocolate chip), take your phone off the hook, turn on some soft music, and settle back for a long, relaxing coffee break. Oh, you should have some Kleenex handy, because I'm going to share with you about spilling and mopping up, trying and failing, laughing and crying.

I want to share Father God's view of a whole world full of people who spill their coffee, and how he feels about stains everywhere.

Messer-uppers and spillers are Father God's favorite people in all eternity! Why? Because his strength is made perfect in our weakness, and his light shines on all the stains in our lives. But then, his precious blood removes them, leaving no trace. He makes us just as though we had never had a mark. He's got a mop-up operation that puts "Mr. Clean,"

"Spic and Span," and even "Fantastic" to shame.

I want you to know Father God in a more special way than you ever thought possible. Is your self-esteem at a low ebb? YOU ARE IMPORTANT TO HIM!

Walk with me and Father God through our exciting adventure of faith. Oops! Sorry about spilling on you again.

> *This is what the Lord says: "Let not the wise man boast of his wisdom or the strong man boast of his strength or the rich man boast of his riches, but let him who boasts boast about this: that he understands and knows me, that I am the Lord who exercises kindness, justice, and righteousness on earth, for in these I delight," declares the Lord.*
>
> *Jeremiah 9:23-24*

The Adventure Begins

Getting to know Father God and developing a relationship with him does not necessarily mean that life is going to be roses and featherbeds. In his omnipotent wisdom, he knows how much we can handle.

This adventure of faith began with the end of my world. I'll never forget Tuesday, November 6, 1979, the day my father went to be with God. I didn't know God was beginning to set in motion a plan for my life that he had formed in his heart for me before the foundation of the world.

I remember running across the parking lot at Central Assembly Christian Life Center in Boise, Idaho, where I worked with my father as his music minister. My heart was beating so hard and fast I could hear it pounding in my chest.

"Oh, Jesus, please, no!"

I rushed past restraining hands into my father's office and stopped short. There he lay on the floor like a fallen giant . . . my daddy, my confidant, my friend.

"It can't be! He's too healthy! He's too young. His ministry is just beginning to explode around the world!"

These thoughts passed through my mind in a jumble as I was gently guided from the room. Outside his office the staff was crying out to God for his healing. I couldn't pray. It was as if my heart were turned to stone and time had stopped.

There had been a special bond between us. I was the firstborn of five children. When I was four, I became ill with rheumatic fever and had to stay in bed for many months. During that long illness, Daddy taught me how to read and entertained me with fantastic adventure stories. He would make trips to the library and bring me back his favorite classics. He seemed to always be ready to talk to his little four-year-old.

There was never a communication problem between us, even in my teen years. I told him everything, even things he probably would rather not have heard.

I became his music minister after graduating from Northwest College in Kirkland, Washington, my parents' alma mater. For nine years he had groomed me, guided and encouraged me in this ministry. He had helped me to develop the music department at Central Assembly into a dynamic tool for the kingdom of God.

Even though I was on staff, I would sometimes sit on his lap, and he would pray away my tears and fears as he would gently rock his beloved girl.

He was my picture of what God is like—gentle, loving, caring, understanding, patient and wise. How could a gentle, loving, caring Father God allow him to die? Daddy had been in the prime of his ministry, and it was reaching around the world.

My father had been a faithful servant and minister for God for nearly fifty years. When different religious "fads" had come along, he had remained steadfast, preaching the solid word of God.

Several years before this fateful day, God had put a special burden for families on his heart. He began to zero in on how much God cares about the family unit. Multitudes of couples were reunited in my father's office, instead of going through the tragedy of divorce.

One Saturday evening, my father was awakened in the middle of the night by giant hands on his shoulder. They raised him to a sitting position, and a deep bass voice told him, "Don't be afraid. I bring you a message from Father!"

Daddy asked who the visitor was, and he replied, "I am mentioned in Luke 1:19." The angelic visitor was there for about four hours that evening.

When he had gone, Daddy looked up the verse in Luke, and read, "I am Gabriel. I stand in the presence of God, and I have been sent to speak to you and to tell you this good news."

Thus began a series of twenty-seven supernatural visitations from heaven with angels, bringing messages from God to remind people in the twentieth century how much Father God cares about the family, about individuals, about you. The message that had the highest priority was the sacrifice of Jesus, and what it means to us. There were no new revelations, but glorious illumination of truths in God's Word.

Daddy was told by God through the angelic messengers to share these truths with his church, and that the Holy Spirit would give the message wings. Daddy obeyed God, and tapes of his sermons began to circle the globe.

The book *Angels on Assignment* was written by Charles and Francis Hunter from tapes of these messages. It has become a best seller of over a million copies and has been translated into seventeen languages. Thousands have accepted Jesus as a result of reading the book, or of listening to the tapes of these dynamic, anointed truths.

And now Roland Buck, pastor of Central Assembly in Boise for twenty-nine years, loved by his congregation, his staff, his family, and respected by the entire community, was gone.

My father's funeral service several days later filled the church as well as a closed circuit overflow auditorium. His many years of faithful service did not go unnoticed; people of all ages, rich and poor came to honor this great man of faith.

Celebration replaced sadness as this became my father's coronation day. All heaven seemed poised, watching, as men and women, teenagers, boys and girls, decided to give their lives to God.

My heart was heavy in spite of the air of victory. And then my Uncle Walt Buck's voice, ringing with triumph, lifted me. He said, "Kids, you haven't lost your daddy! Congregation, you haven't lost your pastor! We know right where he is!"

What a beautiful reminder of a truth that was part of the foundation stone of my father's faith. A truth that had been illuminated through the angels. The truth that God is righteous, which means he has the unfailing ability to always do the right thing by you. Nothing that comes into any of our lives comes as a surprise to God. He knows the exact need of each and every one of us. He simply asks for our childlike trust in his unfailing ability to care for us.

My little family of four stood together as my father's earthly form was laid to rest. God knew it was best at this time that we didn't know we would soon be thrust into an adventure that would totally change the course of our lives. I had no way of knowing that what looked like an ending of a ministry, was the exciting beginning for Alan and me, and our two children.

I went home rejoicing, in spite of my tears. I knew where my father was, and my heavenly Father knew where I was.

> *My frame was not hidden from you when I was made in the secret place. When I was woven together in the depths of the earth, your eyes saw my unformed body. All the days ordained for me were written in your book before one of them came to be.*
> *Psalm 139: 15-16*

Portrait of a Coffee Spiller

I like to know a little about the people I'm reading about, so here are some highlights about my family and a little background on how I became a spiller of coffee in my life.

My mother Charm is a spunky, redheaded Norwegian and Roland, my father, with his dark, wavy hair, looked like Paul Newman. My parents were both ministers, and their influence and faith are intricately woven into the tapestry of my life.

I joined them ten months after they were married. Daddy picked out my name, Sharon Rose. Three years later, my wriggly, red-faced baby sister Charm Lorraine was born. I initiated her into the family by giving her a rip-roaring case of measles.

When I was five, God blessed our family with a little boy. He was named Terry Lee. We only had

Terry briefly. Crib death claimed him when he was six months old. My father shared with me through his tears that Father God could see the whole picture of Terry's life.

He had let us have him for a little while, but then, maybe, he saw some great hurts in Terry's future. In his love and mercy, God took him home to heaven to grow up so that he would be spared those things. Wow! The first brick in the foundation of my faith in Father God was cemented into place. Through this tragedy I began to understand.

When I was eight, my brother Ted Alan was born—big and hungry. He weighed ten pounds and was twenty-four inches long. Today, he's six feet, five inches tall. Two years later, my little sister Marilyn Kay, "Mimi," came along, making our family complete.

Now back to Sharon Rose, the coffee spiller. I was ill with rheumatic fever through many of my growing-up years. So, while my mother was taking care of my sisters and brother, my Daddy became my best friend, story-teller, and teacher. I wanted to be exactly like him.

I did not have the "preacher's kid" syndrome. I felt privileged being a "P.K." and meeting all the evangelists and singers who came through. Dad did not put pressure on us to be what everybody else thought we should be. Whatever we did or did not do was based on both of my parents' personal convictions.

In Junior High, I had a Christian teacher for history who had one of the longest faces and saddest spirits I had ever seen. He was always scolding me for laughing all the time and being so happy.

One day in exasperation he said, "Sharon, what would your father say to all this laughing? After all, he is a minister." I remember looking up with my eyes dancing and saying, "My dad laughs too!" My poor teacher shook his head in wonder at Christians enjoying themselves so much. What a shame that people have a picture of Christian life as pious and joyless.

Everyone in my family is an excellent athlete except me. I was born totally uncoordinated. My life was greatly complicated while I was growing up by my lack of coordination combined with nearsightedness. Vanity kept me from wearing my glasses in public.

Combine lack of coordination with nearsightedness, stir in great enthusiasm, and you get a lot of bumps and bruises, and become great at original apologies.

To top it off, I have no sense of direction. I get lost whenever I drive anywhere new because I have a hard time with right and left, north and south, and maps. I lose my car in parking lots, and provide entertainment for people trying to help me with whatever I have lost. It's fun though, because I'm a people person and have made some wonderful new friends while tracking down my purses, keys, cars, and places.

I've always loved to write. In college the guys found out writing poetry came easily to me. I was besieged with requests for "custom-made" poetry for girlfriends.

Oops, I Spilled the Coffee Again!

As far back as I can remember, music has been a part of my life. In my preschool years, I would line up my dolls on chairs and direct my "choir" vigorously. Music has always been the way I have expressed my deepest feelings about Father God.

My only problem is that when I sing, inside I'm throwing my head back and belting out my music with great gusto and soul, but what comes out is a sweet, light soprano. I'm easy listening on the outside and black soul gospel on the inside.

Even though there's not an ounce of "soul" in my entire body, I continually give it "one more try." My son walked in on me one day, listened a moment, and shook his head. Putting his arm around me, he said kindly, "Give up the soul singing, Mom. Lots of people like the way you sing now." The music I was able to get out of my choirs helped make up for what my voice wouldn't do.

Inside, I feel very cool and sophisticated, with a touch of mystery and intrigue thrown in. Outside, I bounce, and in the middle of being cool, I blow it by forgetting and being enthusiastic. Being a forgetter makes it tough to fight or argue with anyone. I'll be mad at my husband Alan, put my nose in the air and resolve not to speak to him until "he apologizes." Ten minutes later, I'm laughing and talking with him, and I suddenly remember my resolve of silence.

If you recognize yourself in any part of this portrait, be encouraged. Our kind of people are here to bring lightness to a world that can get pretty serious. Our childlike wonder and joy keep our spouses and children from getting in a rut. To top it off, think how good we make almost everybody else look. In the next few pages I hope you laugh your socks off at the delicious sense of humor our Father God lets his people enjoy, as we laugh at ourselves. All this, plus the tender, holy moments of his love.

The reason my heart is filled with inextinguishable joy is that God loves me just the way I am. In his kingdom, and as part of his great team of believers all over the world, I am delighted he needs a blonde forgetter, spiller, joyful, bouncy collider, exactly like me.

We are all valuable to God no matter who we are or what kind of personality we have. We are each a unique, one-of-a-kind creation. There's nobody in the whole world exactly like us. And even if you don't know Father God yet, he already has a spot in his big heart with your name on it.

> *I call you by name and bestow on you a title of honor though you do not acknowledge me. I am the Lord, and there is no other; apart from me there is no God. I will strengthen you though you have not acknowledged me.*
> *Isaiah 45:4b-6*

Resurrection Power

I am the "Eternal Optimist." I wake up every morning happy and excited about life, anticipating a glorious day. I always expect the best from people and circumstances. My father encouraged my joyful attitude. When I came on staff as his music minister, he constantly reminded me that my joy and sparkle were my greatest assets in working with people. Although I could have been intimidated by the gaps in my musical training, Dad simply wouldn't allow it. He would tell me to let the joy of Jesus flow out of my life and surround myself with helpers who could make up for what I lacked in the technical area.

This approach worked; as a result, our music department was dynamic and filled with hundreds of young people, singing their hearts out for Jesus.

Oops, I Spilled the Coffee Again!

In the days following my father's death, however, my light went out. My tears flowed almost of their own volition. I lost weight because I couldn't eat. The doctor gave me pills to help me sleep. It seemed as though my mother Charm and my brother Ted were doing beautifully. They had been unanimously elected co-pastors of this thriving church. The confidence and faith they had in God at this time was supernatural evidence of his love and care. My sisters Charm and Marilyn outwardly also seemed to be doing well in handling their grief. So, my mask went on.

It was a cold January day when my mother and I boarded a plane headed for Virginia to keep a speaking engagement my father had made before his death. I was going along to sing and keep my mother company. During the flight the Lord spoke to my heart to write a book about my father. I told him I had no idea even how to start. God told me he would help me, and over the next few months I sensed his guidance.

Another step in the unfolding of God's destiny for me had begun. I was busily researching my father's life. In doing this, I felt like I had stabilized from the grief of his passing. Life was back to normal.

Then one day while I was playing racquetball with a friend, Ricki Carr, my heart suddenly began to pound in my chest. Cold sweat broke out, and I had a flashback of my father's death. I could see him vividly in my mind's eye, lying in his office like a fallen giant. This flashback, which came without warning, took my breath away.

From that time on, this happened over and over again. It was always unexpected and produced the same feeling of terror I felt when I actually saw my Dad lying in his office. I could be happy and talking with a friend or enjoying time with my family, and this heart-stopping flashback would occur.

I didn't tell anyone how I was feeling. I lost my sparkle, my joy, and my zest for living. My music ministry, my relationships, and even my marriage were affected. The plans for my book lay idle. There was no way I could concentrate on writing, with my nerves in such a state.

During this time our family went to Disneyland for a week's vacation. I relaxed a little, but even "Mickey Mouse" couldn't help me. A week after our return, I was back in my distraught state. Outwardly I was humorless and tense, but everyone passed it off as stress. This all happened about six months after my father's death, and I thought I should be getting over it. Was I going crazy?

In late March of 1980, Terry Law, president and founder of Living Sound International, a music group that God had used in a tremendous way behind the Iron Curtain, came to minister in Boise. Terry had been a good friend of my father. Daddy had received some exciting prophecies about Terry's ministry during the angelic visitations. The prophecies had happened just as God had said, and this had confirmed in Terry's heart the validity of the messages my father had received from heaven.

Oops, I Spilled the Coffee Again!

Alan and I had lunch with Terry the day he arrived. Terry had no idea of my state of mind, and we laughed and talked and had a wonderful time of fellowship. Terry told us to be sure and come to his service that evening, because God had given him a real "Barnburner."

What a service! The church was filled with people praising and worshipping the Lord. Terry stood up suddenly and went to the podium. He said, "This has only happened about four times in my many years of ministry, but God has spoken to my heart not to preach tonight. Instead, I want us all to imagine we are in the throne room of heaven and begin to praise God around the throne."

I immediately pictured my father in the throne room. I dropped to my knees and cried to God, "Why is he there, and not here?" The torment I had been going through the past months was unleashed in a storm of sobs. I cried and cried with my head hidden in my arms . . . alone.

When the service was over, I asked Alan if we could leave as quickly as possible. When we got home, I again had the same flashback, along with the tortuous feelings that always accompanied it. I had finally shared with Alan what I had been going through, and his response had been to love and cherish me. That evening as my body shook with nervous chills, Alan didn't know what to do except to pray and hold me close.

Sleep finally came in the wee hours of the morning. But when I woke up, I felt exactly the same as I had the night before. I thought, "I can't take this anymore!" Suddenly, before I could cry out to God for help, I felt a sensation like cool oil starting at the top of my head and flowing through my entire body, untying every knotted nerve, unloosing the tenseness. This was followed by a flood of exhilarating joy.

I leaped out of bed and went to the mirror. My face looked different. My light was back on. I looked out the window, and the sky looked bluer, the grass greener. That morning I knew once again what it felt like to be born again! My shoulders felt so light, released from the heavy burden of grief I had been carrying. I felt like I could fly. I was like a butterfly that had burst forth from the heavy wrappings of a cocoon.

Alan knew immediately that something had happened to me because I laughed at his silly jokes again. During the past months, I had lost my sense of humor. I didn't say anything to him about what had just occurred, however, because I was afraid this feeling of freedom and release would go away like it had just a week after we had returned from Disneyland.

I deliberately thought of the scene in my father's office that had been producing such agony of mind, and God had supernaturally removed the sting. It was wonderful. I was healed!

Staff members told me later that when I walked through the office doors at the church, they knew something had happened to me. My face looked different, much more relaxed. My brother Ted met me and said "Sharon, you've come just in time. Terry is on the telephone for you from the airport."

Surprised, I took the phone. Terry told me that as he was getting ready to board the plane, the Lord spoke, telling him he couldn't go until he called me and gave me the message the Lord had given him for me the night before. Terry said he had looked all over for me after the service but wasn't able to find me.

I asked, "Terry, what was the message?" Terry replied, "Sharon, the Lord told me to tell you he has seen your grief for your father, and he is going to fill that void with his own presence."

I shouted, "Terry, he already has!" I shared with him what God had done that morning. "Terry, I'm glad you didn't find me last night. Maybe I would have thought that what happened to me this morning was in response to what you had said. Now I KNOW this is a supernatural touch from God!"

My heart overflowed with love for Father God as I realized how much he personally loved me, to touch my life with his resurrection power.

His glorious, life-changing power exploded through eternity the day Jesus rose from the grave, and two thousand years later it has not lost one atom of power. Over and over again God unlooses that tremendous force to touch individuals and reverse the negative in their lives.

That power is there for you, just for the asking. It's there in your grief, your joy; in any nervous, mental agony, and in your emotionally-drained state of mind. God wants you to know he's waiting to liberate, restore, revitalize, and redirect. This power is at your fingertips. It can be released in your life by simply expressing your need to Father God.

> *The Spirit of the Sovereign Lord is on me, because the Lord has anointed me to preach good news to the poor. He has sent me to bind up the brokenhearted, to proclaim freedom for the captives and release for the prisoners, to proclaim the year of the Lord's favor and the day of vengeance of our God, to comfort all who mourn, and provide for those who grieve in Zion—to bestow on them a crown of beauty instead of ashes, the oil of gladness instead of mourning, and a garment of praise instead of a spirit of despair.*
>
> *Isaiah 61:1-3a*

It Wasn't the Pizza

"God, you've got to be kidding!" Sleepily I rolled over and snuggled up. It was nice to have such warm, cozy feelings in my heart for God and to be so relaxed. As I lay there in the middle of the night, I thought how exciting the day had been for my whole family. The copy of my first book, *The Man Who Talked With Angels*, had finally arrived. To me, thumbing through the pages was like gazing at my newborn babies for the first time.

My kids and my husband all felt part of the thrill. My daughter Angie and son Terry had done their part by helping with housework, being quiet (as possible), and trying not to interrupt when I was writing. My husband Alan had been my partner all the way, encouraging me, telling me when the chapter I was writing was awful, editing, and cracking the whip to keep me going when I needed it. Alan had even washed and folded clothes, and had sewn on buttons during this time. It was wonderful!

We ordered our favorite food that evening to celebrate my book finally being published—Pizza! It was hard for everyone to settle down and go to sleep, but we finally got the kids to bed and hit the sack ourselves. I yawned, "God, I need to sleep. This is a busy time for me." I had continued working as music minister after my father's death, and Easter was our next major production. We were working on a beautiful musical. Alan was also on staff at Central Assembly heading the tape ministry. His talents as an excellent artist were being used, and he was working with me in the music department as sound engineer. Life was wonderful and warm fuzzies were floating all over the place. "Good night, God." I drifted off again.

Suddenly the room was alive with heaven's electricity. I was jolted awake as God very definitely spoke to me again. "Sharon, I want you to resign your music ministry and go out and continue to share the truths I made so real to your Dad!" I knew then I had eaten too much pizza. This must be indigestion.

But just in case, I very carefully said, "God, if this is you and not the pizza, may I remind you that I

don't speak in front of people!" This was true. In all
the years I worked with my father, he could not pay
me enough to give any kind of talk. I could yak
forever to my friends. In fact, my daughter nick-
named me "Yakky Doodle." She used to tell people,
"My mother was born in Yakima, that's why she's so
yakky!" It was one thing to introduce a song the choir
was doing, but I wouldn't even give a talk in staff
meeting once a month.

"I helped you write a book, and you had never
written a book before, Sharon."

"Well, Lord, that's different."

"Is it?"

Oh, this must not be pizza. Pizza doesn't give
you goosebumps and butterflies. I tried one last argument. "Lord, I'll have to ask my husband first."

"That does it," I thought to myself. "Alan
would never want to do something like this."

I wondered why the Lord smiled and said,
"Good night, Sharon. Sleep tight." Did he know
something I didn't? I was to find out very soon.

The next morning after the kids had gone to
school, I shared with Alan how the Lord had spoken
to my heart. "There's no way, is there, Alan?" I asked
hopefully.

I was startled to see the tears begin to stream
down my husband's cheeks. Of all things, God had
beat me to him. Alan began to share with me how for

the past several months God had been dealing with his heart about the same thing. He said, "Sharon, remember when Gabriel visited Dad in his office and how Dad told us that Gabriel always reflected the joy that is the atmosphere of heaven except that one time."

Daddy had told us that on this particular visit Gabriel was very sober and paced back and forth in my father's office. Finally, Daddy felt like it was all right to ask Gabriel why he appeared to be so concerned. Gabriel told him that God was concerned that after this beautiful visitation from heaven, people would respond for a season to the challenge and the truths God had made so alive, but then they would forget and go back to sleep. Daddy had shared with us that he had fallen to his knees before God and promised him that as long as he had breath, he would not let people go back to sleep.

Alan said, "Honey, I know God wants us to go."

I said, "I'm scared!" I had a lot to think about that day. How could God want someone like me to go out and speak? What about the tremendous responsibility in sharing this dynamic message? The message included God's love and care for the family. How the family is the closest thing on earth to the heart of God. How in this day and age, when the devil is bringing his heaviest artillery to bombard the foundations of the home, God knows what is happening. He feels the tremendous hurts of people as wives leave husbands and husbands leave wives, and the remaining partner is crushed. He sees children who are battered and brokenhearted. He sees the rebellion as parents and children turn away from each other.

The message brought by the angelic messenger to my dad was one of reconciliation and restoration for families. Also included in the messages from heaven were many truths about the nature of God as expressed through the sacrifice of Jesus. There were beautiful messages on the Atonement, on the Blood of Jesus, and on the Power in his Name.

I wondered why God would send out a spiller, a person who always forgets her purse, can't tell her right from her left, and continually gets lost. Then the perfect argument hit me. "God, how am I supposed to get started? Do you want me to send out a resumé to let people know I'm available?"

I'm not sure, but I think I heard God chuckle as he said, "Sharon, let me handle that!" Two weeks later the phone rang. It was my friend Kay Becker. She and her husband Jack had been youth pastors at Central Assembly but had felt the call to start a church in Ontario, Oregon. Central Assembly had helped mother their church, Christian Life Fellowship, which had grown to over 600 people for Sunday morning worship. Kay had called to ask me to speak for the ladies' fellowship. She told me it was time for me to start speaking and had her arguments lined up to talk me into it.

Oops, I Spilled the Coffee Again!

She was talking so fast she didn't hear me say, "Okay, I'll come and speak." She kept on trying to talk me into it. "Kay, I said yes!"

She paused in amazement, "You did?"

"Yes, I did." Then I told her how the Lord had spoken to my heart and that she was the first call I had received. Kay was excited and agreed with me that I'd better do what God had put on my heart to do. Time to warm up your coffee. We're getting into the good stuff!

For it is God who works in you to will and to act according to his good purpose.
Philippians 2:13

God's Yakky Doodle

As my mother and I drove the sixty miles to Ontario, Oregon, several weeks later, I clutched my stack of notes as if my life depended on it. I had practiced my talk on Alan, and he had passed it with a "7." But the real thing was coming up faster than I could believe.

There were about eighty happy, chattering ladies in the auditorium when we arrived. I couldn't laugh or talk. My mouth was dry and my breath was coming in short gasps! I knew by the way my stomach was knotted that I would have an ulcer by the end of the evening.

The preliminaries seemed to last forever, but finally I was introduced. My knees knocked as I walked to the podium. My hands shook and I dropped my notes! When I retrieved them, some of the pages were upside down. Horrors! I knew I had heard God wrong.

Surely, he never intended one of his kids to go through this torture! I cleared my throat and decided to pray first. After the "Amen" I took a deep breath and delivered my hour-long talk. Indelibly imprinted on my mind is the sight of those women with their eyes getting bigger and bigger, leaning forward to catch every word that came from my lips. And do you know why? When I finished, I sat down and looked at my watch. I couldn't believe my eyes. Including the prayer, I had given an hour long talk in exactly fifteen minutes. No wonder the listeners had leaned forward so intently with their eyes popping. They had never before heard anyone talk that fast. My words must have come out like speeding bullets.

I was humiliated. I said, "God, what's going on here? How could you let this happen to me? I thought you were the one who set this up."

I had received an envelope from the hostess when I had first come in and had tucked it in my purse. Now I opened it to find a nice honorarium for speaking to the group. "I have to give this back, Lord. I didn't earn it!"

The evening ended forty-five minutes earlier than was planned. During the dismissal prayer, I kept my eye on the door so I could sneak out at the "Amen." I was making a beeline for the exit when a lady grabbed my arm, startling me out of my socks. With tears in her eyes, she threw her arms around me and said, "Oh, Sharon thank you. You shared just what I needed to hear."

"I did?"

Then more ladies gathered around and expressed how the Lord had ministered to them.

"He did?" I was shocked.

The topper came when the local president of Women Aglow, an international organization of Christian women, asked if I would be available to speak for Women Aglow the following month. I told her my schedule was quite open at this point. I couldn't believe what was happening. God had touched people in spite of me, an imperfect vessel. I was glad I hadn't been too hasty about returning the honorarium.

Then my friend Wanda Lehmkuhl came running up to me. She had been pianist for my choir for four years before moving to Ontario. She gave me a hug, and told me how great I had done. "Sharon, I was proud of you!" Wanda had always been one of my biggest fans.

I said, "But, Wanda, didn't you notice how fast I talked?" She laughed and said, "That's for sure. Nobody dared move in case they missed something." Then she gave me some great advice. "Sharon, God has given you the gift of gab. Your nickname isn't Yakky Doodle for nothing. Use the gift God has given you when you speak!"

Later that evening, after mom and I had blown some of my honorarium at Wendy's (I was starved because I was too nervous to eat before the meeting), the Lord spoke to my heart about his responsibility and mine. "Sharon, all I'm asking for is a willing vessel. It doesn't matter if you say a little or a lot if I'm lifted up. My part is to meet the need of the hearer."

Wow, talk about taking off the pressure. He isn't looking for someone who is a fantastic speaker, or tremendously educated, or polished. He's looking for people who are willing to say "Yes."

This truth was beautifully illustrated during the time the angels visited my father. He was impressed one night to write a message from God in the first person. The reference in the Bible, given to him by the angel, was Exodus 31:1-6.

This talked about the time the Lord had given the people his plans for building his temple. Exodus speaks about the Lord giving the people the abilities to do different things.

In down-to-earth, twentieth-century language, listen to what Father says to us. "The Lord speaks now to you. All your life forces are in me. Your drives, your talents, your skills. As you commit yourself wholly, even your potential springs from me.

"Bring these words to the world. I have loved you. I have cared for you. Yes, I have planned your steps, and when you would yield, have directed your path.

"Your successes come from me. Your wealth has come from my hand. Your creative skills and your abilities to succeed are because of me. Because of your failure to recognize me and walk in my ways, you have limited the Lord your God. Your life has been restricted so that you have not known its potential. As you make him Lord of all, he will also be Lord of WHAT YOU CAN BE, NOT ONLY WHAT YOU ALREADY ARE!"

Wow! These are tremendous words from Father. To me the most special part of this promise is that as we give him all of us, he'll help us to develop the hidden talents inside that we have been afraid to expose in case we should fail. We don't have to settle for being what we already are. In each one of us, there are exciting, unexplored possibilities waiting to burst forth. And God has promised to help us begin! You can't ask for any more than that. In my case I haven't stopped talking about how wonderful Father is since he began to unloose the potential that lay dormant inside this Yakky Doodle.

Because of your partnership in the gospel from the first day until now, being confident of this, that he who began a good work in you will carry it on to completion until the day of Christ Jesus.

Philippians 1:5-6

35

Handmaiden

The engine on the big jet roared. Alan and I looked at each other in anticipation of a glorious time together in St. Louis, Missouri.

When the Lord asked me to go out and speak, I had no idea that my third speaking engagement would take me out of Idaho, and that Alan would be able to go with me. When I had received the phone call from Gwen Shaw, founder and president of the "End Time Handmaidens of the Lord," an international intercessory prayer group, I told her she was probably looking for my mother, Pastor Charm, who is an experienced speaker.

Gwen said, "That's what I thought, Sharon, because I've heard her and she's excellent. But when we went to the Lord about this, He impressed upon us that

He meant you. You are his handmaiden for this meeting."

Needless to say, I got goosebumps and shared with Gwen how the Lord had been leading me. But I told her I was nervous about anyone paying my expenses to go so far when I was so inexperienced. Besides, the convention would fall on our wedding anniversary. I hated for Alan and me to be apart.

Gwen didn't even hesitate. "You must bring your husband along, dear. This will be a special time for all of us."

I told her then that we didn't have any extra money to pay for Alan's expenses to come with me, even if all my expenses were paid. Gwen told me that God wanted us to come, and he was big enough to take care of the expenses.

I thought about my first speaking engagement several weeks before, and how I had felt about returning the honorarium when I thought I had failed. This trip would be a much larger investment by this organization. The responsibility began to really shake me up until I remembered that I was to be the vessel, and it was God's responsibility to meet the needs of the people.

I took a deep breath. "Gwen, if God wants Alan and me to go, we'd better do it."

Alan and I stepped out of the airporter and looked up at the largest Marriott hotel we had ever seen. As we looked around, we noticed everyone was wearing a special badge. We decided there must be another group meeting in the hotel at the same time.

Suddenly, a lovely lady came rushing up to me, and gave me a big hug. "You must be Sharon. I recognize you from your picture on the book." She turned to Alan, "And you must be Alan."

Alan answered dryly, "I'd better be."

Our hostess laughed and told Alan to go register while she took me to meet Gwen and to see where the meeting would be held.

I was totally unprepared when we walked into the huge convention center. I knew that it was going to be a larger meeting than the other two, but I had thought in terms of several hundred people. There were flags from all over the world hanging everywhere. There were book tables, record tables, and what looked like hundreds of chairs. What had we gotten into?

Before I could ask, an exquisitely-dressed lady stood to greet me. My hostess introduced me to Gwen Shaw. Gwen made me feel honored as she told me how glad she was to meet me, and how much she would have enjoyed meeting my father. She was a beautiful and gracious lady.

Then she totally won my heart as she hugged me and our tears mingled. She shared how much my father's ministry had meant to her and to her organization. Then she told me there were about fifteen hundred people already registered for the convention, but they were expecting two thousand the next evening when I was to speak.

Oops, I Spilled the Coffee Again!

I squeaked, "Two thousand?" I felt faint. She went on to tell me that this convention included missionaries from many nations because this was the Handmaiden's International Convention. I would be sharing the platform with Phil Driscoll, one of the greatest trumpeters in the world.

As Alan and I walked to our room in stunned silence, we were greeted with hugs and tears by many people who had read my father's book and mine, and had been blessed by them.

There was one young woman about my age whose husband had been killed in a tragic car accident the year before. She had been left with three young children to raise. During her time of grieving, someone gave her my book. Reading it had steadied her faith, and turned her heart upwards to a loving, heavenly Father who cared for her, knew her by name, and had everything in control. Her testimony was a blessing to Alan and me.

When we finally got to the privacy of our room, we looked at each other in dismay. "Alan," I cried, "what are we doing here? Two thousand people, Phil Driscoll! This is only the third time I've ever spoken. I'm scared." Alan was not a big help. He was scared too, but he did his best to encourage me.

That night at dinner we were impressed by the caliber of Christians in this group. We were excited to meet a woman who was an administrative assistant to one of the members of the President's Cabinet.

Another woman was a successful attorney from the East Coast. There were many successful business people and missionaries from around the world. It was exciting to meet all these precious members of God's family.

The first evening's service was tremendous, and the music was fantastic. Alan and I were both refreshed in our spirits.

A prayer meeting was scheduled for the next morning at 6:30. Alan and I decided we needed to go. Our past experience with early morning prayer meetings had led us to expect only a few of the most spiritually hardy people. We were amazed to find at least 800 people already in deep intercessory prayer when we arrived about 6:45. Many were on their faces before God. The power of these united prayers reached out in waves as we were walking down the hallway. It was dynamite.

Following prayer, Gwen taught a Bible study on the fruits of the Spirit. She shared a special truth she had found in her research. Included in the fruits of the Spirit are patience and long-suffering. Her research showed patience as MARRIED to poise. She enlarged on this truth by sharing that as believers, we could have Holy Spirit Poise in our life as a fruit of Jesus dwelling within.

The light came on in my spirit. I prayed, "Lord, if I've ever needed Holy Spirit Poise, I need it now."

Oops, I Spilled the Coffee Again!

There was standing room only in the convention center that evening. Phil Driscoll was tremendous as he played his trumpet and sang. The Holy Spirit Poise that I had been wearing all day slipped a little, and I told Alan, "I can't go up there and speak and sing after Phil Driscoll."

Alan looked me in the eye. "Nonsense, Sharon. You are going to do what God told you to do."

One of the characteristics of a charismatic convention is a total disregard of time. I was all right until one hour passed, then two. My Holy Spirit Poise began to slip a little more. Gwen noticed and whispered not to worry about time. "We have all night," she said. I decided if she wasn't worried, then I wasn't going to be.

Finally, it was time for me to be introduced. As I was walking to the podium, the pastor who had been the MC for the evening stepped up to me. He was visibly moved and trembling. He told me, "Sharon, when you stood up, it was as if my eyes were opened. I saw a huge angel standing with you. He's standing here now."

Talk about Holy Spirit Poise! I walked up to the podium with confidence and authority, sensing the hosts of heaven in attendance.

My husband sat listening with his mouth hanging open in amazement, as the power of Father God took control of my message. Alan knew something supernatural was happening as he watched me boldly stand before the largest audience I had ever faced. I sang and shared the glorious works and visitation of God with no stuttering or fear, but with God's power and anointing.

When I had finished, a holy silence filled the room. People had been boisterous in their praise, but now there was an awesome stillness as a sense of the Holiness of God filled the room. Then people began to fall on their faces before him.

The pastor who had been weeping and praying throughout my message told me God allowed him to see the angel standing behind me while I was sharing. The visible presence of one of the angelic hosts was confirmed by several people who told me that while I was speaking it was like I was standing in front of a huge light.

I felt so unworthy and yet so honored that God would manifest himself in such a special way. Alan and I sensed we were on Holy Ground that evening. We felt as though our lives would never be the same.

Needless to say, the next morning when we flew out of St. Louis, I was ready to take on the world. I was ready to go straight from the airport to my fourth speaking engagement, which was a women's brunch.

I walked through those hotel doors in Boise into the meeting, and lost all semblance of my Holy Spirit Poise. I could hardly put a sentence together. The Lord wanted me to know that he was the one who gave the power. On my own steam, I would fizzle.

Oops, I Spilled the Coffee Again!

The ladies decided they loved me anyway. Whew! God still accomplished something special for the Kingdom. And I hoped that I had learned where my source of strength and power lay.

> *For God, who said, "Let light shine out of darkness," made his light shine in our hearts to give us the light of the knowledge of the glory of God in the face of Christ. But we have this treasure in jars of clay to show that this all-surpassing power is from God and not from us.*
>
> *II Corinthians 4:6-7*

OOPS

Oops, I Spilled the Coffee Again!

God continued to open doors. Alan and I finally realized we had to obey the direction we had felt from God seven months before. We resigned our positions on the church staff, and Alan began to freelance as an artist and sign painter.

We were booked solid through the summer of 1982. Our last meeting was scheduled in August in a little church that met in a converted garage in Yakima, Washington.

Seating space was so limited, the fire department allowed only a specified number of people in the church at a time. Therefore, the pastor announced this meeting was by reservation only. So many reservations were requested that it was necessary to schedule three services. When these reservations were full, the pastor had to tell people, "Sorry, it's too late."

Every service was packed to the doors. During the last service the doors were opened, and chairs set outside. The temperature was 104 degrees in the shade, and the little church did not have air conditioning; instead, electric fans were blowing. Through the open doors in the front, you could hear sounds of traffic, including an occasional motorcycle roaring by. Behind the church was a doghouse full of newborn puppies. Through the open door you could hear them yipping, accompanied by the howls of the mama dog. In spite of these distractions, God was there in a beautiful way, and lives were encouraged and changed.

One of the people who called in for reservations was my cousin Don Ward. He was excited about my speaking in Yakima because it had been through my Dad's book, *Angels on Assignment*, that he and his family had come back to God. He wanted his wife Jan and two children, Steven and Annie, to meet me. My book had clenched the things God had done in their lives.

Don hadn't seen me in years, so he was upset when he called in for reservations too late. There were no more seats available, even for cousins. I knew nothing of this, so I was surprised when I received a call from Don a few days after the meeting. He said, "If I can get enough places in Yakima for you to speak, would you come back again?"

I said I would.

Two days later Don called me back. I hadn't told him how many places were "enough," so he had gotten busy. From a Sunday through a Wednesday he had scheduled twelve speaking engagements. These included three on Sunday, a breakfast meeting, luncheon, three TV shows, three radio shows, and three evening services. I had Thursday off and a final luncheon on Friday. He asked me, "Is that enough, Sharon?" When I regained consciousness, I assured him that it was more than enough.

Don called a number of businessmen in the area to see if they would help with funds for publicity while I was there. One of these men was the host of the most popular radio talk show in the area. His format was much like Phil Donahue's.

When Don called him about helping publicize my meetings, he asked if I would be available to be on his show. Don shared this with several Christians in the area. They felt uneasy about my being on the show, because they weren't sure if I could handle this man's razor-sharp wit. Don called and gave me the invitation but shared the concerns of these people.

My brother Ted, Alan, and I talked this over and asked the Lord about it. We all felt that if God had opened the door, then he could handle my walking through it.

The radio program was scheduled for early Monday morning. It was a beautiful Indian summer

Oops, I Spilled the Coffee Again!

day in Yakima. I dressed in my sophisticated, "dress-for-success," navy blue suit. My makeup was perfect, and for once my hair turned out just right. With my briefcase in one hand and my matching blue shoulder bag, I looked like the businesswoman of the year—if you couldn't hear my knees knocking.

I was determined to give the host of the show a good impression of Christians. I would show him how "together" I was. I looked so businesslike and proper, even my husband was in awe. As I walked into the impressive building which housed the radio station, I squared my shoulders, clutched my brief-case, and with my schedule for the day firmly in hand, marched forward. Christians were praying all over Yakima that God would be with me on this program.

After a short wait, we were introduced to the host of the show. He seemed genial and was dressed in a beautifully tailored and expensive-looking suit. He asked me if I would like a cup of coffee. I gratefully accepted. He brought me the cup, and Don, Alan, and I made small talk with him. Suddenly my papers slipped out of my hand. Without even pausing in my conversation, I bent to pick them up. I forgot I was holding a full cup of coffee, and as I bent down the coffee bent with me. There was coffee every-where, on the host's expensive suit, the floor, my papers, and me. I was more than embarrassed. I was mortified. I remember muttering to God, "How could you let me do this? I wanted him to think I was organized and efficient for You!"

The secretary ran to get paper towels. The host mopped himself up while she and I worked on the rug. Even one of the disc jockeys got in on the clean up. I couldn't help but notice his flaming red hair worn in an Afro. He was as cute as could be.

The atmosphere had been stiff and formal when we first came in, but as we worked together on my spilled coffee, the ice was broken. Soon we were laughing and talking like old friends. The "Miss-Dress-for-Success" image lay buried beneath mounds of soggy paper towels, and my more normal, friendly self emerged. By the time we were dried off, my butterflies were gone, and I could hardly wait for the interview to begin.

As Alan and I walked into the studio with our host, we became aware of the familiar, tingly feeling of heaven's electricity. We knew the hosts of heaven were settling in to watch the action, and provide the help that might be needed.

And there was action! As we began the show, the Holy Spirit took control. Several times as the show progressed, the disc jockey with the flaming red Afro tiptoed past the door, giving me the thumbs up sign and mouthing, "You're doing great!"

During the first half hour, the host asked questions that opened the door for me to share Jesus in a fantastic way. During the second half, the host fielded phone calls, even answering them in a way that uplifted the Lord. He hung up on several crackpot questions.

Anyone tuning in would have thought it was an exciting, dynamic Christian broadcast. Afterward the host told me he didn't know what happened. "I had planned to play the devil's advocate." He said. "I was going to really nail you, but I didn't!"

The disc jockey who had encouraged me said, "I want a copy of that book! I want to know more about this."

Once again the tremendous, enabling power of God was illustrated through a spilled cup of coffee and a willing vessel. It's also interesting to me to note that he wasn't about to let me be anything other than what he made me to be. He didn't let me be "cool."

For we do not have a high priest who is unable to sympathize with our weaknesses, but we have one who has been tempted in every way just as we are—yet was without sin. Let us then approach the throne of grace with confidence, so that we may receive mercy and find grace to help us in our time of need.

Hebrews 4:14-16

Let Me Call You Sweetheart

My husband, Alan, is one in a million. He teases me that when I was born God said, "Oh, oh, I'd better get busy and make a boy baby fast who can handle this one!" Nine months later Alan was born.

What a joy he is. We've been married over twenty years, and we are still each other's biggest fans. I tease him that he married me because I laughed at all his jokes. I honestly think he missed his calling as a stand-up comedian.

He is a fantastic artist and makes our living by sign painting and free-lance art. His fine art reminds me of Norman Rockwell.

When we were courting, he was gone for eight months training at boot camp. He wrote me every single day, sometimes twice a day. On almost every envelope he would draw a detailed cartoon. He always sent his letters to my job, so I wouldn't have to wait until I got home from work to read them.

The mailman was so excited about his drawings on the envelopes, he would dig them out and show them to the other postal workers. When I told Alan about this, he began to draw a cartoon series about mailmen on the envelopes. They loved it.

The sense of humor we share has helped us over many bumps in the road, and Alan learned before we were married how much he would need it in living with a forgetter-spiller.

We hadn't known each other very long before Alan told me he was marrying me. I was so over-whelmed and so much in love with him, I was almost speechless. He didn't find out until after we were married what a Yakky Doodle I am.

Soon after we were engaged, some friends of the family came to visit from out of town. I couldn't wait to introduce my fiancé to them. I took him by the hand and proudly said, "I'd like you to meet my fiancé, uh, uh," and my mind went blank. I could not remember his name. Mother saw my predicament, slipped her arm around my waist, and whispered softly, "It's Alan, silly." I don't think Alan or my friends realized my lapse of memory. They thought it was love.

Alan would never have known, but I couldn't resist giving him a card I found the next day. On the outside it said, "Let me call you Sweetheart." Inside it said, "'Cause I keep forgetting your name." Twenty years and many forgettings later, we both still get a good chuckle out of this incident.

Speaking of names—I went to Northwest College with my best friend, Jan (Wingett) Finke. (Unfortunately for all of us Seahawks fans, this was long before their training camp was at Northwest College.) As we were moving into our room on that beautiful campus, there was a knock on the door. A lovely blonde dressed in lavender came in and introduced herself as our next door neighbor. She said, "My name is Sharon Rose Hoskins." I responded, "You're kidding! My name is Sharon Rose Buck."

Another knock on the door, and a dark-haired girl with a big smile walked in saying, "Hi, I'm Sharon. I live across the hall."

I said, "My name's Sharon, too. Meet Sharon, our next door neighbor."

Before the day was over I had met at least ten Sharons. I told my roommate, "Jan, I'm not going to be one of the masses of Sharons."

Jan agreed with me and said, "But what can you do?"

I got a flash of inspiration. "I'm changing my name right now. From now on I'm Roni, and that's how we'll introduce me."

So Roni was born. Jan and I had our picture taken, and put it on our door with a sign, "Jan and Roni." There was a reception for new students that evening, and we were given name tags. I put "Roni

Buck" on mine, and was introduced to the staff and faculty by that name. Several of the Sharons I had met said, "I thought your name was Sharon."

I said, "Too many Sharons; I'm Roni now."

I signed all my papers, and enrolled in all my classes as Roni, and after several days no one even remembered Sharon Rose. The only problem was MY memory. At first people thought Roni was stuck-up because I would never answer the first time my name was called. It wasn't long until I adjusted.

Imagine the surprise of my poor father when he called to see how I was getting along and was told there was no Sharon Buck registered on campus. He said, "There has to be. She's my daughter, and I personally delivered her to the school!" He was told there was absolutely no record of a Sharon Buck.

Then someone remembered, "There is a Roni Buck."

Daddy thought for a moment, then laughed, and said, "That's my daughter."

Psychologists tell us that names are very impor- tant to people. If you don't remember someone's name, it gives them the feeling they aren't important enough to be remembered. On the other hand, it gives people a tremendous sense of self-worth when their names are remembered.

Throughout the Bible God often talks about names and their importance. Psalms 147:4 says God even has names for all the stars. "He determines the number of stars and calls them each by name."

In Isaiah 49:16 God says, "See, I have engraved you on the palms of my hands." We are so valuable to him that he's inscribed our names on his big hand. This is so he can look at each of our names every once in a while and say, "That's my kid!"

If your self-esteem is a little low because of circumstances that have come into your life, let the following story of my dad sink deep inside your heart as a reminder that God knows your name. My dad was in his office on a Saturday studying for the service the next day. He had shared with me that he probably would not have any more visitations from the angels because the message God wanted to remind the world about was complete. But six weeks before my father went to be with the Lord, God added a beautiful postscript.

As Daddy was studying, the angel Gabriel appeared to him one more time. He brought a beautiful message about God's love and care for individuals. While Gabriel was talking with him, the phone rang. When Daddy answered the phone, there was a little lady on the other end of the line who needed help badly. She was having financial problems, and her husband was very ill. She told my father if he saw any of the angels, would he ask them to ask God to give her some help. She didn't tell my father her name.

Oops, I Spilled the Coffee Again!

As my father was talking to her, Gabriel said, "Tell Bonnie Thompson that God has already heard her cry, and the answer is on the way." When daddy shared this with her, she shouted with joy because God knew her name. What made this even more special was that Bonnie had not been called by this name since she was a little girl. It was the love name her mother had called her some seventy years before. Nobody else knew her by that name, but God did. And to let her know how much he cared for her, he called her by that name which for her had special meanings of love and tenderness.

Mother met Bonnie later. Her husband was well, their financial problems had been helped, and Bonnie was telling anyone who would listen to her that God knows people by name. This wonderful story is for you. God wants you to know that he knows your name. He loves you, and he has room for you in his big family.

If the Lord delights in a man's way, he makes his steps firm; though he stumble, he will not fall, for the Lord upholds him with his hand. I was young and now I am old, yet I have never seen the righteous forsaken or their children begging bread.
Psalm 37:23-25

Gliding Is Where It's At

"Please mother, would you take us?" My daughter Angela was pleading with me to take her and her friend Tammy Purdy to the Blanche Evans Modeling Agency. They both had dreams of a glamorous modeling career. I decided it would probably be fun and might encourage the girls in their eating habits. Blanche Evans would let them know exactly what is involved in being a model. I was sure french fries and

Cokes were not included, even in a teenage model's diet.

Blanche is a lovely woman whose beautiful complexion and trim figure seem ageless. She is always exquisitely dressed and made up to perfection. Her grooming is faultless. Her hair, however, is the most brilliant shade of red I have ever seen. The girls were overwhelmed, and so was I.

She was gracious and kind to them, and soon they were asking all kinds of questions. Much to my delight, she confirmed that french fries were out for models. She told the girls they were both lovely, and had them walk for her. Blanche told them about her finishing school for teenagers, which could lead into serious modeling as they grew older.

I was caught off guard when she turned to me and asked, "Sharon, have you ever thought about being a model?" I was shocked. Never in my wildest dreams had I ever even considered modeling. Blanche continued, "Why not? How tall are you?"

My height of 5'6" was a little short, but when you model for a photographer, it doesn't matter. My size eight figure also pleased her. I was flattered, needless to say.

Blanche called a couple of times during the next few weeks, but I was in the process of finishing my first book and we never made contact.

Several months later, my book was completed and in the process of being published. I had resigned my music position to respond to the doors the Lord had opened, but most of my speaking engagements were on weekends, leaving free time during the week. Late one night I remembered Blanche asking me about modeling. Why not check it out? Modeling sounded almost too glamorous and fun to even be right.

When I called Blanche the next day, she told me she was in the process of starting a class for gals my age. The goals for the graduates of this class were modeling for department stores around town, taping local TV commercials, and being photographed for special ads for flyers and newspapers. There were to be five other girls in the class.

When the big night came for my first class, I dressed in my favorite outfit, fixed my hair, and did my makeup with the greatest of care. I was ready to be launched into a new career.

When I arrived at the school, there was only one other person in the reception room. She was simply dressed, almost to the point of being dowdy. She wasn't very pretty, until she smiled. When she smiled her whole face was transformed. She smiled and I smiled back, but I noticed her looking me over. I sensed she felt a little intimidated by the way I had gone all out for the evening.

She introduced herself as Ann and told me she was a secretary. She had just gotten off work. Ann was so friendly and unassuming, I felt a kindred spirit.

Soon we were chatting like we had known each other all our lives.

Blanche was in her office talking with one of her graduates, a model who had dropped in unexpectedly from an assignment in Italy for the European Vo*gue*. A half hour passed, and finally Blanche walked out with a tall, extremely thin girl with a mass of thick, blonde hair. She was gorgeous. She hugged Blanche and walked out, leaving her with the two of us.

Blanche stared after her former student for a moment, and then looked at her two rookies. She took a deep breath and sighed. Squaring her shoulders, she had us come into her office so she could show us pictures of the model who had made it. I could tell Ann and I were quite a comedown from the aura of glamour the model had left behind.

Blanche decided she might as well come back to earth to the two of us who were waiting so eagerly for an exciting new career. She looked at me and whispered, "Sharon, you'll have no trouble at all." She looked at Ann and sighed softly under her breath.

"First of all, girls, I want each of you to walk in front of the TV camera so we can videotape you. This will give us an idea of where we need to start."

I thought to myself, "Oh, this is a cinch," and jauntily walked across the mirrored room. Ann, her shoulders slightly hunched, sort of shuffled timidly in front of the camera.

Blanche's hair seemed to turn a shade redder. "Oh, girls! No! No! No! Oh my, the first thing we have to do is teach you how to walk properly. Sharon, what a swing. Shame on you. And Ann, you walk like a ninety-year-old lady!"

Blanche played the videotape of our respective walks back for us. I was thoroughly embarrassed as I saw what my walk really looked like. Ann and I both giggled nervously as we viewed her shuffle past the camera.

Blanche proceeded to show us how to walk correctly. It looked so easy. She had a beautiful fluid walk. She told us, "I think of a song, and walk in time to the music."

The first song that came to my mind was the currently popular "I Listen to the Trumpet of Jesus" by Russ Taff and the Imperials. I began to walk to that exciting beat.

Ann said, "Blanche, I think I've got it." Blanche said, "Yes, you do, Ann, you're doing much better. That's it! But Sharon, what on earth do you think you're doing?"

"I'm walking in time to the song in my head."

"What on earth are you singing?"

I proceeded to walk and sing the song.

Blanche's face turned pink. It looked nice with her bright red hair. "No, no, Sharon. You must glide, like this." Again she walked smoothly and gracefully across the floor.

I said, "What about this song?", and sang a few bars of David Meece's "We Are the Reason."

"That's a little better," she replied, "but don't you know the Vienna Waltz?"

I did, but it seemed a little slow after "Trumpet of Jesus."

Ann was gliding all over the room. Personally, I thought she was showing off a bit. Blanche clapped her hands. "Wonderful, Ann, you've got it! Sharon come over here and watch Ann."

Ann very patiently tried to show me again, and again. I couldn't help but giggle. Even the Vienna Waltz didn't help.

Blanche's face now matched her hair. "Sharon, anyone can glide!"

I said nervously, "I guess I may be the exception that proves the rule."

Blanche said, "Come on, girls, let's leave Sharon's walking for a moment, and I'll show you the basic routines used in variations by all models." She showed one routine a couple of times.

Ann practiced a few minutes and said, "Blanche, I think I've got it." And she did. The two of them began to do the routine all over the room.

I tried my best, but finally Blanche said to me as kindly as she could, "Sharon, this doesn't come naturally to you, does it?"

I said, "No, I guess it doesn't. I'll practice some more."

An hour and a half later I finally mastered gliding. Ann had learned to glide, picked up three routines, and was fast becoming teacher's pet. She told Blanche, "I'm forty, and I've been feeling dowdy. I'm ready for a change in my life. This is really going to be fun!" Blanche was excited about Ann. With her big smile and terrific moves, she wouldn't be dowdy very long with Blanche working on her.

Blanche turned her attention back to me. She sighed again and said, "Both of you come to my office and we'll talk." Ann, sparkling with her success and no longer intimidated, skipped along. I continued to glide, so I wouldn't forget how.

Blanche told us that her models were the best in Boise after graduating from her school. Then she looked at me. I was sitting checkbook in hand, waiting to write a check to pay for the course. She refused my check saying, "Sharon, let's consider tonight on the house. Perhaps you will want to go home and think about this a little more."

I couldn't believe my ears. I had failed modeling school after only one lesson. I made up my mind not to tell anyone, even my husband. But when I got home, I forgot and blurted out the whole story to Alan. He threw back his head and roared with laughter until the tears streamed down his cheeks. "It isn't funny," I said pouting.

That set him off again. When he could finally speak, he said, "Honey, I wondered about your taking modeling, because you are so totally uncoordinated.

But you were so excited, I didn't have the heart to say anything to you."

I said, "Alan, I didn't know it took coordination to be a model."

He burst into laughter again. "Sharon, I can see you trying to glide to 'The Trumpet Of Jesus.' Think of it this way. You learned how to walk correctly, and it didn't cost you a dime!"

There's a wonderful lesson to be learned from this story. When our walk before God becomes imperfect and difficult, he doesn't lose patience, nor does he write us off as being unable to make it. Instead, he puts into force all the provisions of Heaven to enable us to walk uprightly.

Christian tradition has God getting mad at us every time we slip up and make a mistake. But a beautiful truth that was illuminated during the supernatural visits from heaven to my Dad is this: GOD DOES NOT RECORD OUR FAILURES IN HEAVEN. Through Christian tradition, it has been passed down that God will forgive you of the sins you commit before you become born again. But after that, watch out! He's keeping track of all the slipups in your life. And one of these days when you stand before God, He's going to pull down a big screen, and shine the light on all those failures.

The exciting truth is that just like Blanche could erase the videotape of my walk and make it just as if it never took place, God does erase our failures and literally destroys the records.

Every time you stumble and fall, simply ask God to forgive you, and he will start a brand new videotape on your life.

He especially wants you teenagers to know this truth. He knows how you go to youth camp and get zapped and feel like you can take on the world. You come home and try, but you stumble. (Adults do this too.) Then because you feel like you have come to God so many times to ask forgiveness for the same thing, you are almost embarrassed to come to him again.

Don't ever be afraid to come to Father God. He doesn't remember all the other times you've come to him. Every time you come, he starts a brand-new page in your life. This truth is liberating! Grab hold of it. You can walk in victory like you've never walked before. You can glide and he doesn't care if you keep time with "The Trumpet of Jesus." He likes it!

> *For I will forgive their wickedness*
> *and will remember their sins no more.*
> *Hebrews 8:12*

The Turquoise Intruder

The heroine of this story is my sister Charm. Through our growing up years, it seemed to me like Charm never got into trouble like I did. I found out later the reason was that by watching me go through all my scrapes, she learned very young when to be quiet.

When I had boy troubles, for instance, I would throw myself across my bed and sob so loudly the whole house would shake. Charm would sit on her bed during misunderstandings with boyfriends, the tears streaming silently down her cheeks. A much more pitiful, but quieter sight than I was.

Charm and I have opposite tastes in clothes. As

a pastor's wife, she has always dressed very graciously in neutral or pastel tones, shades which are very complimentary to her coloring. I have always been one for more splashy, bold colors.

Charm needed a new outfit for General Council, which is the annual international meeting for ministers and missionaries from the Assemblies of God Church. I was visiting her, and we decided to go shopping in Spokane, Washington, for her new outfit. When we walked in the door of Frederick and Nelson, a gorgeous turquoise dress called to me from the back of the store.

"Charm," I said, "There's your dress!" We rushed to the dress, and at my insistence Charm tried it on.

She said, "Wow, Sharon, it really is turquoise, isn't it?"

I yelled, "It's perfect, Charm! It makes your eyes look turquoise."

Charm said, "I'm surprised you can even see my eyes."

I told her confidently, "Sis, Bryan will love it." (The magic words)

Charm hesitated. "You know Sharon, Bryan really likes me in pink!"

I said, "Oh, he's seen you in pink lots of times. He'll love you in this dress. He won't be able to help himself."

Charm couldn't resist my enthusiasm and purchased the beautiful turquoise dress.

Alan and Bryan were watching a football game on television when I burst in ahead of Charm and began to extol the wonders of the gorgeous new dress *we* had found.

"Well, let's see it," Bryan said.

Charm was a little reluctant to model it after my buildup, but she finally put it on and walked into the room.

Alan said, "That's very nice."

Bryan said, "Wow, it sure is turquoise, isn't it?"

Charm asked Bryan, "Do you like it, honey?"

I interrupted, "I love it. You guys do too, don't you?"

Bryan said, "I guess I'm used to Charm in more subdued colors."

Alan added his two bits worth. "I kind of like to see Charm, but with that dress on all I can see is turquoise."

Bryan gave Charm a hug. "If you like it, honey, keep it."

Charm answered as all wives through the ages answer that kind of statement. "You don't like it, do you? I want to wear something you like."

I said, "Well, I think it looks great on her. Come on, Charm. Let's go hang it up."

When we got to her closet, however, we were

totally amazed at what occurred. When Charm hung up that bright turquoise dress, all the pastels in her closet gasped and fell off their hangers.

This homey illustration reminds us that we are all individuals. I liked the turquoise dress so I thought my sister would like it too.

Isn't it great how Father God created such variety in people. We don't have to be afraid to be ourselves. From all walks of life and from different backgrounds, Father invites all kinds of people to join the family. And when one of us throws off our filthy rags and puts on the new garment of righteousness provided by Jesus, it's the grand finale of all shopping trips.

This garment is absolutely free, purchased at a price that stripped heaven of its most valuable treasure. Jesus purchased it for us by offering his undying soul as payment for our ugly, awful, filthy, garment of sin. The stroke of God's judgment struck Jesus so that every one of us might be clothed in his righteousness.

Isaiah 53:10-11 says, "Yet it was the Lord's will to crush him and cause him to suffer, and though the Lord makes his life a guilt offering, he will see his offspring and prolong his days, and the will of the Lord will prosper in his hand. After the suffering of his soul, he will see the light of life and be satisfied; by his knowledge my righteous servant will justify many, and he will bear their iniquities."

When we put on the righteousness of Jesus, all God sees when he looks at us is Jesus.

By the way, Charm exchanged the turquoise dress and got a lovely pink and gray suit.

> *I delight greatly in the Lord; my soul rejoices in my God. For he has clothed me with garments of salvation and arrayed me in a robe of righteousness, as a bridegroom adorns his head like a priest, and as a bride adorns herself with her jewels.*
>
> *Isaiah 61:10*

Speaking of Mr. "T"

I happened to see Mr.T the other day on TV. He was glittering with his special trademark of pounds of gold necklaces. I read that he has four hundred in his collection. He is definitely worth his weight in gold. But the thought struck me that Mr. T's gold necklaces have nothing on God's fantastic jewelry. Let me explain.

My father was extremely protective of his girls. Since I was the oldest, I paved the way for my sisters in the area of dating. After the first one, it's much easier for fathers to relax a little.

Alan had come to our church as a result of tracts being passed out on the streets in Boise by our church youth group. He was in town with the National Guard, and when he received one of our tracts, he and his friend decided to visit the church.

When we began dating, my father was very concerned about who this young man was. Daddy didn't feel a bit hesitant about calling Alan's parents and his pastor to see what kind of person he was. At the grand old age of twenty, I was quite resentful of my father's checking up on Alan. I felt I had good judgment.

I remember sitting on the lawn of the parsonage at 534 Federal Way. It was a beautiful spring day. The grass had been freshly cut, and the fragrance filled the late afternoon air. I told my father how I felt about his checking up on Alan.

Daddy took the steam right out of me when tears began to roll down his cheeks. He said, "Sharon, God gave you to me and you are my treasure. To me you are like a beautiful, priceless pearl necklace. I wouldn't leave my most treasured necklace lying around for just anyone to pick up." My tears mingled with his as I threw my arms around his neck and thanked him for caring so much.

What a beautiful picture of my Heavenly Father my earthly father gave me. He made it so easy for me to love God, because of the way my father reflected his nature.

As I've traveled around, however, I've realized one of the greatest needs people have today is to recognize God as Father and realize how valuable they are to him.

Isaiah 62:3 talks about how we are God's crown, a precious possession that he holds carefully in his hand. If you are feeling low and unimportant, you need to know you are so valuable to God that he wears you as a crown on his head.

A young girl who had been in my choir for many years experienced Father God in a very precious way. Sandy had been a Christian since she was a little girl, but she never had real victory in her life. She constantly went through ups and downs in her walk with the Lord. Nobody knew why.

After her graduation from high school, she decided to give six months to Youth with a Mission (YWAM). In September she went for training in Hawaii. During the first part of her training, she was involved in a series of studies on openness and brokenness. God began to show her the bitterness in her heart that she had toward her parents ever since she was a child. Sandy knew she had to deal with this bitterness, especially her feelings toward her father. She realized that through the hurts she had experienced as a child she had build up walls of resentment in her life that only God could break down and heal.

Oops, I Spilled the Coffee Again!

This had happened through many misunder-standings that had come about as a result of her over-hearing her parents say that if her sister had lived, Sandy would never have been born. She didn't hear the rest of the conversation in which her parents expressed to each other how very glad they were that God had given them Sandy.

Sandy's sister had been a little lady, and Sandy had always been a tomboy. She is an excellent athlete and a star basketball player. After hearing only part of the conversation between her parents, Sandy began to think of herself as a poor substitute for her sister. For fear of being rejected, she also became unable to tell her parents she loved them. She developed a resentment against her father for not attending any of her sports events or anything that was important in her life. She felt he used his poor health as an excuse. The final straw was when he did not attend her graduation, even though she was valedictorian.

During the final night of the series on openness and brokenness, Sandy felt she needed to respond and to be upheld in prayer. She hesitated because there seemed to be so many other people in need. Finally, one of the workers told Sandy that she felt impressed that Sandy needed to go forward for prayer, for God had a special message for her. Sandy went forward.

After all the others had been prayed for, one of

the ministers came and told Sandy God had given him a special message for her. He said, "Sandy, God wants you to imagine you are sitting on his lap with his big arms around you. God says, 'Sandy, I've seen how hurt you were when your earthly father wasn't able to attend your basketball games. But I, your Heavenly Father, was there. I was at all of your games, cheering you on and watching you intently. I was always proud of you. When you graduated vale-dictorian, I was there. I have always been there. I love you, Sandy, and when you have done wrong I have forgiven you. You must also speak of forgiveness to your parents.'"

That night in Boise, Idaho, the phone rang in Sandy's parents' home, and they heard those precious words for the first time in years, "Mom, Dad, I love you!"

Sandy shared with me in a tape that she felt like a hundred-pound weight rolled off her shoulders as she forgave her parents, and said those words to them. She has experienced new victory and stability in her life since getting to know God as Father. God wants you to know that even if you never knew the love of your earthly father or mother, he loves you more than they could ever begin to love you. Included in that love is forgiveness through Jesus.

Because Father forgave us, He's asking us to

forgive and be restored in our relationships to parents, children, and spouses. His ultimate plan for our lives is reconciliation and restoration.

> *This is how God showed his love among us: He sent his one and only Son into the world that we might live through him. This is love: not that we loved God, but that he loved us and sent his Son as an atoning sacrifice for our sins. Dear friends, since God so loved us, we also ought to love one another. No one has ever seen God; if we love one another, God lives in us, and his love is complete in us.*
>
> *I John 4:9-12*

Turn This Thing On!

Through the pages of this book I've been sharing over and over that Christians need to learn to laugh at themselves and not get uptight about life.

My father had the opportunity on several occasions to visit heaven. One of the things that impressed him was that while he was in the presence of God, God told him to relax because God already knew everything about him anyway. Father told me that he could hear the angels laughing, and that the very atmosphere of heaven is joy. There is a noticeable absence of piety.

One of the beautiful truths that God illuminated to my father through the visitations of the angels was that even in times that look so bleak to us, God's glory floods the earth. He reigns and is in control at all times.

As music minister for many years, I have many examples of times I have had to laugh at myself. The choir members will never let me forget one Christmas dress rehearsal.

Christmas fell near the weekend that year, so there were going to be many people leaving town who wouldn't have the opportunity to see our Christmas presentation. We decided to invite the public to our dress rehearsal. Members of our congregation were encouraged to bring their friends. We were pleasantly surprised to have a large crowd of people at our rehearsal.

We had forgotten, however, to hook up a light for my music stand. The problem was solved when someone found a huge flashlight, which I held in my hand to see my music. This worked very well until I began to get inspired. I forgot I was holding the flashlight in my hand and began to direct with both hands, really getting into the music. This caused the light to flash all over the platform. I am an extremely aggressive director.

I was concentrating so hard I didn't realize what I was doing, and began to get a little perturbed by the snickering in the choir. They all managed to get themselves under control, however, until we came to a deeply moving part of our program where I was to share with the audience.

I went to the front of the platform and began to talk into my mike. I couldn't understand why people weren't responding. Then I realized I didn't have any sound. I tapped the mike and said to Alan in rather unspiritual tones, "Would you turn this thing on?"

I noticed at this point several people in the audience nearly fell off their seats with laughter. Now I knew I had to get that mike on and recapture the mood we were setting. I tapped the mike again vigorously. "Honey, I need this on!"

Alan threw up his hands and shook his head. I finally looked down at my mike. I was still holding the flashlight. I had to laugh at myself and it gave me a great opportunity to share the same thing I'm sharing with you.

This is a beautiful illustration of a very important truth the Lord gave us. He said we can talk forever, but our sound doesn't matter if our light is turned off. He urges us again and again to let our lights so shine before men that we don't need to say a word.

Oops, I Spilled the Coffee Again!

      All that light shining from our lives is the Glory of God on display to a dark world. Wherever we go the world around us should light up because we are reflecting our Father.

> *This is the message we have heard from him and declare to you: God is light; in him there is no darkness at all. If we claim to have fellowship with him yet walk in the darkness, we lie and do not live by the truth. But if we walk in the light, as he is in the light, we have fellowship with one another, and the blood of Jesus, his Son, purifies us from all sin.*
>
> *I John 1:5-7*

> *Whoever claims to live in him must walk as Jesus did.*
>
> *I John 2:6*

The Highway Patrol and Grace

I was starved for pizza. Alan had to work late, so a couple of friends and I decided we would go out and get some. Alan had our good car and had warned me not to drive the old Dodge. The desire for pizza overcame Alan's instruction, and throwing caution to the wind, I took off in the Dodge.

I had lost my contacts earlier that week, and a new pair was on order. Without my contacts, I was careful not to drive too fast. I didn't want to get stopped. Imagine my horror when I looked in the rearview mirror and saw the flashing red lights of the highway patrol. I pulled over and waited for the policeman to come to my window. My heart was pounding. The verse "Be sure your sins will find you out" came floating across my conscience.

Oops, I Spilled the Coffee Again!

I rolled down the window, and the patrolman asked for my driver's license. Oh, no! I had changed purses and had forgotten to put in my license. I told him this with my voice quivering a little and asked him why he stopped me. He said, "You were going too slow. Don't you know that's just as dangerous as going too fast?"

I blurted out, "Oh, I was trying to be careful because I lost my contacts."

"And you're required to wear them while driving, right?" he asked. I could have bitten my tongue.

"They're on order, though, Officer." He just looked at me, shook his head, and began to write.

"Do you have your registration?" I hadn't been stopped before so I wasn't sure where it was kept. He helpfully told me it might be in the glove compartment. Relieved, I opened it. Empty! Very quietly he wrote again.

Next he said, "I notice your safety sticker is expired."

I gulped, "It is?"

He went to the rear of the car, wrote down the license number, and went to his car to call it in. He seemed to be gone for a long time. My friends sat in silent judgment.

The officer came back to the window, and said soberly, "The license plates on your car are expired."

I said, "They are?"

He continued, "They are not even for this car.

They are registered to a car belonging to Rev. R. H. Buck."

I was trembling now as I remembered Alan had hung those plates on the car so he could drive it to take care of all these things that needed to be done to it. I told the officer this and that Rev. Buck was my father.

The policeman said very solemnly, "Young lady, do you know I have just listed eight counts against you?"

I gasped, "Officer, my husband specifically told me not to drive this car, but I wanted pizza so badly that I did it anyway. I'm sorry! I've learned my lesson, and my husband is going to be really upset when I bring all these tickets home."

The officer looked at me again and put his head down on my window. Then he looked up, shook his head, looked me right in the eye, and said, "Sharon, I'm not going to give you a ticket for these eight violations, although you deserve it. You are to forget your pizza and just go home! Go straight home. I'll be following you. Remember, no pizza!"

I was shaking like a leaf as I drove home. My friends were amazed at the turn of events, and I think they felt I should have had at least one ticket. I was aware that I had experienced the grace of man in action.

But how much more is God's wonderful grace! What an illustration of what God does for each and every one of us! We all deserve God's judgment, but instead he provides his grace.

From the beautiful visitations of angels to my father comes this beautiful illumination of the Scripture found in Ephesians 1:4: We all deserve God's judgment, but instead he provides his grace. As the fire of God's judgment struck Jesus, who offered himself as a sacrifice for us, a cloud ascended that covered all time and all space. This cloud spread out from Calvary on the wings of grace until it stretched backward across the ages, erasing all the charges against man since the beginning of time. Jesus' sacrifice completed the plan to make us all acceptable in God's sight. This is his wonderful, glorious grace.

Grace is one of the most precious words in Scripture. In the time of Jesus, the Greeks were lovers of beauty. Anything which called out of the heart wonder, admiration, pleasure, or joy was designated by their word for grace. Grace also came to signify the doing of a favor graciously and spontaneously, a favor done without expectation of return but arising only out of the generosity of the giver.

Romans 5:20 talks about grace abounding. Again, the original Greek translation carries the idea of abundance that is more than enough. Kenneth West in *Golden Nuggets from the Greek New Testament* beautifully captures this verse in his translation: "Where sin existed in abundance, grace was in superabundance, and then some more was added on top of that."

There's enough grace in God's heart to save and

keep saved forever every sinner that has ever or ever will live, and then enough left over to save a million more universes of sinners, and then even more grace on top of that.

God's grace provides salvation that is shockproof, stainproof, unbreakable, and all sufficient. This grace is ours through the sacrifice of Jesus for us all.

> *Therefore, since we have been justified through faith, we have peace with God through our Lord Jesus Christ, through whom we have gained access by faith into this grace in which we now stand. And we rejoice in the hope of the glory of God.*
> *Romans 5:1-2*

> *But God demonstrates his own love towards us in this: While we were still sinners, Christ died for us.*
> *Romans 5:8*

A Little Squeak

Alan and I had been on the road for about a year and a half. After I had started accepting speaking engagements, the doors kept opening and we kept going through them. Suddenly, we realized that we had lost a year and a half of our children's lives. We had left them with Grandma Buck, adding some spice to her life. Using Grandma Buck's home as a base, we came and went on a regular basis.

But it wasn't the same as our own home, and the children seemed to age at an accelerated speed. All of a sudden Angie was fourteen and Terry was thirteen. We decided we had better check our priorities.

Oops, I Spilled the Coffee Again!

Alan and I hadn't meant for this to happen. We were just trying to follow the Lord. We needed to learn another lesson, which we are still trying to learn to this day. Not every door that opens is a door God wants us to walk through. He says in his word to "Count the Cost."

As I write this chapter, it is out of a heart that has experienced Satan's attacks against the family, the closest thing on earth to the heart of Father God. The messages of God's concern and care that he sent down through the angelic visitations have been a message of faith and trust in Father God. Alan and I have been reminded over and over again that we are more than conquerors because our Father has already won the battle. The joy that I have been writing about has been tested, and, readers, it is real. It's not a joy like the world gives, but it is an inextinguishable, unshakable joy that doesn't depend on circumstances.

Like many families in this time when Satan would seek to deceive the very elect of Christ, Alan and I have made the choice to trust Father God to help us to have his ideas and direction in taking care of some of the poor choices we made in trying to follow him.

Readers, we have seen God at work in our lives. Based on experiencing his supernatural power, We Will Shout To The World, "OUR GOD REIGNS AND YOU CAN TRUST HIM TO ALWAYS DO THE RIGHT THING BY YOU."

My Dad always told people not to say "if only," but instead to say, "but now!" Our "but now" was to load the kids in the car during the summer of 1982, and take them with us to California to the meetings we had scheduled for the summer. We didn't expect five meetings to cancel. Nor did we expect to run into the back of a car in heavy traffic outside San Diego. We did expect the kids to love a summer traveling with Mom and Dad.

Nothing was as we expected. Halfway through the summer, we sent two bored teenagers back to Grandma's house to be with their friends and attend summer youth camps.

We were sad, but Father God once again manifested himself in our need. We had an unscheduled service with a pastor who told us that his congregation was encouraged by the message I shared. We were blessed, because God gave him a word for us. He didn't know that we were worried about our kids, but Father God told him to tell us that they were going to be all right. Father God had everything under control.

After California we decided that since most of my future meetings were in the Seattle area, we would move our family to Seattle. Alan would get a full-time job, and I would go out only on weekends. Most of the churches and Women Aglow meetings where I was scheduled to speak were within a three-hour radius from Seattle.

Again, we thought the kids would love moving

to an exciting big city, but such was not the case. They had never lived anywhere else. They had always gone to the Christian school founded by Grandpa Buck. Life for them had never been anything but living in Boise. They did not want to move.

But move we did. What an adventure! Alan stayed behind in Boise to finish up some business, and made preparations to get our belongings from storage where they had been for over a year since the selling of our house. I was elected to find a place to live and get the kids started in school. They would go with me on weekends, until Alan could come.

We found a cute apartment in Kirkland, Washington, across the lake from Seattle. At first we slept in sleeping bags on the floor. We borrowed a card table from relatives, bought paper plates, imported our TV, and purchased a telephone. We had set up housekeeping.

The first day I took the kids to school, I got lost. It took me two hours to find my way home. I was nearly in tears. For the next two weeks, I got lost every time I left the apartment.

When Alan joined us, we had to move because the apartment was too small. We tried to find a house in the same school district, but we couldn't find one in our price range. Our kids, who had never moved before, moved twice in a couple of months. They were miserable without their friends. It was especially hard for them on weekends to go everywhere with us.

One amusing thing happened that we all laugh about now. Angie was in the ninth grade and hated taking P.E., a required subject in her school. She decided not to fool around going through channels about this. She wrote President Reagan, asking him to excuse her from P.E. In the letter she stated she didn't think a kid should have to take P.E. if she didn't want to.

During this time, I decided to look for work to help us out from under the tremendous financial burden of having been on the road. After years of work that often involved me at nights and on weekends, I decided I wanted to live a normal nine-to-five life for a change. But my job search led to dead ends.

Interviewers liked me, but everywhere I went it was the same story. As one office manager put it, "I really like Sharon, but I closed my eyes and tried to imagine her typing and working with our CPAs, and there is no way I can picture it." Why couldn't they understand that a little routine and structure was exactly what I wanted.

One Sunday I was scheduled to speak in Goldendale, a city about a six-hour drive from Kirkland. I would spend the night there, do a local TV show, and return on Monday. I wanted Alan to go with me, but he couldn't because of his new work schedule.

It was a gray, blustery and stormy morning when I left Kirkland and pointed the car toward Goldendale. I felt resentful and alone. The wind was blowing so hard I was afraid it would blow me off the road. In my heart I was pulling back from the ministry God had allowed me to be a part of. God had continued to bless my ministry as he promises. God's word doesn't return empty but accomplishes what he desires (Isaiah 55:11). But I wasn't seeing the results I had when I was *Red Hot*.

I began to talk to the Lord as I drove. "Lord, how come you're not helping me find a job. All I want is to be a normal human being and live like everybody else."

I know the Lord has a sense of humor because as clear as a bell I heard him say, "Sharon, you've never been normal before. Why start now?"

I had to laugh. I said, "Lord, I'm tired of feeling like a little squeak in the ministry."

Quietly the Lord replied, "Do you mind being a little squeak for me?"

The tears began to flow down my cheeks as I said, "I'm sorry, Lord. I'm giving my ministry back to you, and I'll squeak as long as you give me breath!"

Needless to say, the rest of the trip the Lord and I had a wonderful praise meeting. My spirit was renewed. The direction the Lord had given me before again became crystal clear. Once again the joybells were ringing in my spirit. My renewed zeal was about to be tested, however. When I arrived in Goldendale, it was about fifteen minutes until the service was scheduled to start. I followed the directions I had been given and arrived at the church to find it totally dark, with only a few cars parked near it.

I held onto my joy with all my might as I got out of the car and walked in. There was no one anywhere. As I stood wondering what to do, a young couple walked in. Was I glad to see them! I said, "Could you tell me where the pastor is? I'm your speaker for this evening."

They looked blank and said, "We didn't know there was going to be a special guest this evening. The pastor didn't announce it this morning."

My heart sank. Just then another man walked in. He was the Associate Pastor, but he didn't know anything about my speaking either. "I'll help you set up, though." he said.

Both men went out to my car and helped me bring in my books and tapes. It suddenly dawned on me to ask if there was another church in town. They told me there was, and the name of the pastor. I had done it again! I apologized profusely to the men as they carried my boxes back to the car. I told them I had a terrible time with directions and often got lost.

By that time it was about five minutes until service time. I raced across the little town and came to a church with all the lights on, cars parked everywhere, and the sounds of vigorous singing coming through the walls.

I was sure I was in the right place. I came bursting in the door, explaining what had happened. People came immediately to help me set up. The pastor, a big Norwegian ex-pro football player, told me the church had been completely full for a half hour, and the people had started spontaneously singing and praising God.

By the time I walked on the platform, there was standing room only. The people were ready. I silently thanked God that because of our time together on the road, I was ready too. We had a fantastic service that night. I shared a little of what God had done for me on the way to the service. I told them this evening marked a new beginning for me in the things God wanted me to do.

As you are reading this, I want to remind you again that our God is a God of constant new beginnings. In our day-to-day routine, we can sometimes feel stuck by our job or the circumstances we are in. But in God, every single day can be a new beginning. The joybells can ring. We can renew the zest and energy for living by his supernatural power. He's just waiting for us to ask.

You will go out with joy, and be led forth with peace; the mountains and hills will burst into song before you, and all the trees of the fields will clap their hands.

Isaiah 55:12

Terry, Do You Know Jesus?

All of us who are raising children wonder at times if anything we are trying to teach them is getting through. God has beautiful promises in his word regarding children. God promises that the things we teach our children about him are going to seep in through their skin. This is because the things of God are responded to by the spirit of each child. God allows the spirit of a child to learn, even when we think the child is not paying any attention. I believe this is why it's so important even for little children to be in the presence of God every time the church doors are open—Sunday morning, Sunday evening, every time God's people meet.

Here are a couple of stories from my own kids' lives, illustrating the power of the presence of God.

Oops, I Spilled the Coffee Again!

When my daughter Angie was three and Terry two, they were taking their Saturday-night baths together, splashing up a storm. All of a sudden Angie said, "Terry, do you know Jesus?" Terry at two, his brown eyes big and serious, nodded yes. Angie said, "Whew, I sure am glad!"

I thought, how precious! Even at that age, Angie was aware of spiritual things. Somehow it had seeped into her spirit that people needed to know Jesus, including her little brother.

That same year once when the kids were running out to play, Angie screeched to a halt with a spine tingling shriek. Terry put on his brakes and ran back to his sister.

"Terry," she screamed, "There's a big spider in the way!"

Angie was deathly afraid of anything that crawled, and boys like Terry loved worms and creepy, crawly things.

Terry squared his little shoulders, and before I could rush in, I heard him say in his little two-year-old lingo, "It's okay. I'll save ya, Angie." Clenching his little fists, he stomped that big spider to death. Then he looked at her with his big, brown eyes and said, "I killed him for ya, Angie." Then taking her hand, they ran out the door to play.

I got misty over that evidence of the love that Terry had expressed for his sister. I have often thought since then that as brothers and sisters in Christ, we need to be sensitive and aware of each other's fears and needs. For people who haven't met God yet, we need to be Father God with skin on, hugging and caring for those who are bruised from the bumps of life.

As I was traveling, a mother in one of my services shared this precious story of the love of Jesus for his kids, young and old.

She told me that once her four-year-old daughter came to her and said, "Mommy, how do I know Jesus is real? I can't touch him. I can't see him. I don't think I believe in Jesus anymore."

The mother was crushed, because she didn't know how to explain the concept of faith to a little four-year-old. Several weeks later the mother was awakened about two o'clock in the morning by her little girl. Her face was glowing as she said, "Mommy, Mommy, I know Jesus is real!"

Her mother asked, "Honey, how do you know?"

The little girl answered, "Mommy, tonight while I was asleep, Jesus came into my room. He woke me up and got me out of bed. Then he took my hand, and we walked around the room together and we talked about a lot of things. Then, Mommy, he sat down on my bed, and he picked me up and sat me on his lap."

The mother and daughter would play a little game together at bath time. After the daughter's bath, the mother would get a big bath towel and say, "Now I'm going to wrap you all around."

The little girl continued, "Jesus sat me on his lap

and wrapped me all around. Now, I know Jesus is real because I talked to him!"

That's how everyone of us needs to see Jesus. He wants us to come as little children with our hurts, our broken hearts, our crushed lives, and let him pick us up, and put us in the middle of his lap so that he can wrap us all around with his love.

> *Then little children were brought to Jesus for him to place his hands on them and pray for them. But the disciples rebuked those who brought them. Jesus said, "Let the little children come to me, and do not hinder them, for the kingdom of heaven belongs to such as these."*
> *Matthew 19:13-14*

> *The Lord is compassionate and gracious, slow to anger, abounding in love .... As far as the east is from the west, so far has he removed our transgressions from us. As a father has compassion on his children, so the Lord has compassion on those who fear him. Psalms 103:8, 12, 13*

Father at Work

"I'm going to the restaurant to get a hot cup of coffee. I'm freezing. Would you call me when the airporter finally gets here?"

I had been waiting for two hours for transportation to the SeaTac Airport in Washington. It was December, 1985, during the cold spell that gripped the nation that year. The planes had been running several hours late because of the icy conditions; so had the airporters.

Oops, I Spilled the Coffee Again!

I had just walked out of the restaurant with my coffee when the airporter finally arrived. I asked the driver if we could make my plane. He smiled and said, "We can only try!"

The airporter was full of passengers who had also been waiting because of the weather. Seated behind me was a Japanese woman who was sound asleep. One of the other women in the vehicle saw me glance at the slumberer and said, "Poor thing, she's been riding this airporter since 5:00 a.m., trying to get to the airport.

Since the ride to the airport would take about two hours, we decided to share with each other a little bit about ourselves. When it was my turn, I said that I was an author, had written a book about my father, and was now traveling, singing, and speaking to churches and women's groups. While I was talking, the little Japanese woman opened one eye for just a moment and then went back to sleep.

We finally arrived at the airport, just in time for me to wait another hour. The Japanese woman stretched and stepped sleepily out of the airporter. She walked to the same airline that I did. She had a different plane, but both of us were going to have to wait.

She introduced herself as Judy and said, "I woke up just long enough to hear you say you had written a book. Would you like to wait for our planes together over some tea? I'd like to find out more about your book." I was delighted to wait with her. I noticed as we walked toward the snack shop that she was wearing a dainty cross around her neck.

I took a deep breath and asked, "You are so bright and happy. Are you a Christian? I noticed your cross."

Judy said, "Yes, and you are too, aren't you?" We both laughed with joy. It is so special the way people in the family of God can spot one another. As we sat sipping our hot drinks (I had coffee, of course), I told her some of the highlights of the truths I was sharing and a little about my father's visitations from heaven. I talked about his book *Angels on Assignment.*

She became excited and began to share about her life. She had been raised Buddhist. When her parents had died, her priest had told her that they must not have been good people because they died so young. She refused to accept this and went into a deep depression.

Out of her darkness she cried out to God, "If you're real, reveal yourself to me!" She told me the depression lifted instantly, and joy flooded her being. She then prayed, "God I don't know anything about you. Help me get to know you."

God loves answering prayers like that. Judy purchased a Bible, and God led her to a Baptist Church where she soaked up truths about Father God. Her family, however, was not comfortable in the Baptist church, so they all began to attend a Japanese Methodist Church. It was a good place, but she wasn't sure the pastor knew Father God the way he had revealed himself to her.

The day before we met, Judy had awakened in the morning with that terrible depression once again settling over her like a dark cloud. In the midst of this she cried out, "God, I'm not going to accept this depression again. Please, send someone to talk to me about you!" With tears in her eyes, Judy said, "Sharon, God sent you to me!"

Wow! Again, that's the kind of Heavenly Father we have. He caused all sorts of delays, ice and snow, just to bring this lovely Japanese lady and me together in answer to the cry from her heart.

From Finland, Australia, India, Tanzania, Africa, Nigeria, New Zealand, Germany—from all over the world, and throughout the United States—I have received thousands of letters and calls from people in response to my book *The Man Who Talked With Angels*. In different ways they have all said the same thing: "Thank you for presenting Father God to us and showing us what he's really like!"

It is often through books and people that Father God shares his nature. Perhaps the following excerpts of letters from people who have been helped as Father God has revealed himself to them in their need will clench in your heart the things I've shared about him.

From Rhode Island: "I was afraid to seek God because of some of the sins I had committed. I thought God must be tired of my confession of the same sins over and over. I now realize God will take me back and wants to finish the work he started when I first accepted him."

A man from the Texas Department of Corrections who is serving two sentences for armed robbery writes: "I've realized that God is my Heavenly Father, and he loves *even me!*"

A young woman from Wyoming shares an experience she had while praying: "I said, 'God, why is it so hard for people to find perfect love that doesn't cause hurts?' A man's soft, gentle voice replied, 'Susie, my love won't hurt you.' I dropped to my knees beside my couch and began to sob. Suddenly all of the hurts and unforgiveness from my past were taken from me.

"I felt like a bird let out of a cage. I ran outside, and everything looked more brilliant and beautiful. Praise God! He knows our hearts and reaches out to our needs. Thank you for writing your book about our Heavenly Father."

From Mexico City: "My heart rejoices! My spirit is lighted from the warm love that emanates from our Heavenly Father. He let me feel his touch. It now makes me glow like a newborn baby. I have returned to my sweet Jesus. I thought God could manage just the same without me. I did not know how important I am to him, how invaluable. And how important and invaluable he is to me. His whole beautiful creation couldn't do without me. What a price he had to pay for us. I am thirty years old and have been in a wheelchair for more than four years. God has forgotten my sins, and even though my legs don't work, I want to run towards him and go all the extra miles he wishes to put on me. I am your new brother in Christ!"

Blazing throughout God's word as part of the beautiful gift of Salvation is the truth that when we accept Christ, the records of our sins are destroyed. We are restored to our original state of innocence, just as though we had never sinned. Our hearts become as clean and white as a new-born baby's. What Satan tried to steal from us in the Garden of Eden through Adam and Eve's fall, Jesus restored to us by his sacrifice.

> *So that you may become blameless and pure, children of God without fault in a crooked and depraved generation, in which you shine like the stars in the universe.*
>
> *Philippians 2:15*

The Last Cup of Coffee

Coffee break is just about over. I hope you've enjoyed this time of refreshment. I know I have. Every time I wrote a chapter, I was reminded again of Father God, and all the terrific things he has done for us.

My dream for you in writing this book is that you understand that God provided a bridge for humanity in the person of Jesus. He came to bridge the terrible gap between God and man. Hebrews 7:16

tells us that he is the Indestructible Christ. "One who has become a priest not on the basis of a regulation as to his ancestry but on the basis of the power of an indestructible life."

There were many priests throughout the years of the Old Testament. There had to be new ones trained all the time to take the old ones' places. But when Jesus burst into this world two thousand years ago, he became the last and perfect Divine High Priest.

When he died on Calvary, Jesus took upon himself the awful, stinking rags of the sins of every person who has ever been born or will be born. He carried the weight of these rags from the pit of hell to Heaven's throne room.

As Jesus slowly approached his Father in Heaven, his Father God, who cannot look on sin, had to turn his back on Jesus. This was the blackest moment of all Eternity.

In the Old Testament Zechariah tells how this event took a glorious turn. He describes how the angel Gabriel stepped forth and, his voice ringing out through the halls of heaven, commanded the awful rags to be removed from Jesus, and the kingly, priestly robes be placed on him. Upon Jesus' head was placed the crown of Holiness, and in his hands were placed all power in Heaven and on earth (Zechariah 2).

At that moment, Father God turned and accepted the sacrifice that Jesus had made for us. The job was completed by the Indestructible Christ.

If you haven't met him yet, pray this simple

little prayer: "Father, I want you to become *my* Heavenly Father. I accept what Jesus has done to build a bridge between us. I invite Jesus to come into my heart and make it brand-new. Thank you for loving me so much. Amen."

You are now part of the Family of God.

I John 1:9 declares, "If we confess our sins, he is faithful and just and will forgive us our sins and purify us from all unrighteousness."

Welcome. I love getting new sisters and brothers. In Heaven right now all the angels are celebrating. In fact, they're throwing a party because of your choice. The most special blessing of all is that you can call God, "Abba, Father," which means "Daddy." I encourage you to find a Bible-believing church and begin to learn more about Father God and the new life you've begun.

I would love to hear from you. It would make my day to know that I haven't spilled all that coffee of my life in vain.

> *For you did not received a spirit that makes you a slave again to fear, but you received the Spirit of sonship. And by him we cry out "Abba, Father." The Spirit himself testifies with our spirit that we are God's children.*
> *Romans 8:15 & 16*

Epilogue

DARE TO DREAM

I think back on all the happenings since I first felt impressed to paint this portrait of Father God. This portrait was not written in rosy circumstances, although it emanates the joy Father God wants us to have as part of his wonderful, liberating power.

At first it was exciting for Alan and me to have the opportunity to be part of the ongoing ministry described in this book. We loved sharing the wonderful truths about the nature of Father God that he illuminated through the angelic visitors to my father.

We had never had the opportunity to travel, and our horizons became much broader as we traveled from Idaho to the four corners of America. We ministered to huge churches with massive congregations, and we ministered to tiny handfuls of people. Always, we felt the presence of the Power Team from Heaven with us. Hundreds of people, young and old, accepted Jesus into their lives. Christians were encouraged and renewed.

We sold our home and most of our possessions and took it for granted that we were following the Father. We didn't realize that we had gotten ahead of him until things started crashing down all around us. We made some unwise decisions that left us with nothing financially and materially. The enemy of our souls shouted with glee as he stomped on the White family and ravaged our dreams.

But that enemy didn't reckon with the foundation of faith and trust that was the cement that held our lives together. Like the apostle Paul in II Corinthians 4:8, we could have said, "We are hard pressed on every side but not crushed; perplexed, but not in despair; persecuted, but not abandoned; struck down, but not destroyed. We always carry around in our body the death of Jesus, so that the life of Jesus may also be revealed in our body."

We received a new depth of understanding for hurting people as we experienced sorrow we never had believed would happen in our lives. Through our experiences we were able to bring healing to broken hearts and lives. We were able to share the love and compassion of Father God as expressed through his great gift of love, Jesus his Son.

In the middle of tears and heartbreak, a glimmer of hope broke through. As I wrote every chapter I knew it was a testimony of joy, not produced by circumstances but through faith and trust in our Father's unfailing ability to always do the right thing by us.

Once again I experienced his dynamic resurrection power. With new energy surging through my life, a radio program was born. "Share The Spirit," a daily five-minute chat over a cup of coffee, is co-hosted with Wanda Lehmkuhl, the lady who had encouraged me after my first speaking engagement in Oregon. We have had the opportunity to share the joy and laughter in serving Jesus, using many of the illustrations in this book. In the middle of a dark world, the light has gone forth over the radio waves, affecting thousands of listeners.

At the beginning of my speaking career I had dreamed about starting a radio program, but I had forgotten that dream when we entered the difficult times I have talked about. I started to feel that the truths shared in this book would never be told. I began to despair, but Father God had a plan.

My dream has been resurrected over the airwaves, and through the printed page. The heart of